# Steffen Eichhorn · Stefan Marquard · Stephan Otto

PURE STEAK

Schiffer Publishing Ltd

4880 Lower Valley Road  Atglen, Pennsylvania  19310

**Originally published as *Steak Pur!* by HEEL Verlag GmbH.**
**Photos:** Thomas Schultze: food photos; Christine Birnbaum: pp. 6-7; Stephan Otto: pp. 8-9, 12, 14-15, 135 top; Bernhard Kuehmstedt: p. 135, portrait of Stefan Marquard; fotolia: pp. 4, 9, 12 (Black Angus, Limousin, Charolais) and 13.
**Cover Photo:** Thomas Schultze
**Design and Layout:** Claudia Renierkens, renierkens kommunikations-design, Cologne
**Food Styling:** Katja Korsawe

**Translated from the German by:** Dr. Edward Force

Library of Congress Control Number: 2011940671

Type set in Function

ISBN: 978-0-7643-3927-1
Printed in China

Schiffer Books are available at special discounts for bulk purchases for sales promotions or premiums. Special editions, including personalized covers, corporate imprints, and excerpts can be created in large quantities for special needs. For more information contact the publisher:

Published by Schiffer Publishing Ltd.
4880 Lower Valley Road
Atglen, PA 19310
Phone: (610) 593-1777; Fax: (610) 593-2002
E-mail: Info@schifferbooks.com

For the largest selection of fine reference books on this and related subjects,
please visit our website at **www.schifferbooks.com**
We are always looking for people to write books on new and related subjects.
If you have an idea for a book, please contact us at proposals@schifferbooks.com

This book may be purchased from the publisher.
Include $5.00 for shipping.
Please try your bookstore first.
You may write for a free catalog.

In Europe, Schiffer books are distributed by
Bushwood Books
6 Marksbury Ave.
Kew Gardens
Surrey TW9 4JF England
Phone: 44 (0) 20 8392 8585; Fax: 44 (0) 20 8392 9876
E-mail: info@bushwoodbooks.co.uk
Website: www.bushwoodbooks.co.uk

# Contents

## SIDE DISHES     124

## Index     

## The Authors     

We heartily thank Weber for preparing the grill.

We would also like to thank the AMA (Agrarmarkt Austria) for letting us use their beef cut graphics.

# Foreword

**Dear Readers,**

Not only do we have very similar first names, we also share a wonderful passion: the love of meat, first-class meat, its preparation and its enjoyment. And this passion has brought us together.

When the idea for this book was born, we met to brainstorm at Stefan's headquarters in Tutzing, Germany. It did not end with just exchanging ideas. In the spring of 2009 we met at Stefan's kitchen; Stephan brought all kinds of meat, and Steffen cooked what the pans held. After preparing the recipes of the most varied classics, we simply wanted to know: Can one make a steak of a shoulder cut? Or of a rump cap? How is it with a flank (bavette) or skirt (onglet)?

So we experimented extensively, with mini-salamis, with octopus legs, with batters, and with various stuffings.

When one wants to prepare one of these extraordinary steak cuts, one does best with first-class meat. Naturally, the meat quality has to be right, even with well-known cuts. A briefly grilled shoulder cut of lower quality will not make anyone really happy. But no fear, even fans of classic steak will be happy, whether with filet mignon, onion, or pepper steak.

Stephan has put together an informative chapter from his unbelievable knowledge of everything that concerns first-class steak. There one can read what one should know about buying and cooking beef and the various cuts of steak. Whoever reads this introductory chapter will have even more pride when preparing their steaks.

This project has given us an unbelievable amount of pleasure, and we hope that a taste of this happy mood will be tangible in the recipes. We hope you have become curious about our somewhat unconventional manner of preparing steaks.

**We wish you much joy in cooking, tasting, and naturally in experimenting!**

Stefan Marquard

Steffen Eichhorn

Stephan Otto

# THE MEAT

# Shopping for the Best

**If your meat dish is going to be successful,
then the golden rule is to choose your product carefully.**

With steaks in particular, this rule has tremendous significance, for in principle there is only one method for preparing steaks—grill them briefly at a high heat. Thus the cooking process will only have a very limited influence on the quality of the dish. Roasted and stewed dishes are cooked over a longer period of time along with the most varied and usually intensely flavored foods such as vegetables, sauces, and spices. Thus a lower quality product can often be somewhat evened out in the final product, which is only slightly possible with steak.

**The most important criteria for choosing meat, the true tests for determining quality are of a sensory nature: Taste, tenderness, and juiciness. These aspects, though, must always be seen in connection with ethical criteria that are reflected in the ecological awareness of the farmer and the ability to trace the origin of the product.**

While one usually has the chance to taste the wine or cheese one is buying, this possibility is only very seldom available when buying meat. It is all the more important that one can trust the seller. Beyond that, it helps to consider the following criteria, which are, quite essentially, responsible for the quality of the meat:

- Genetics
- Feed
- Butchering Age
- Aging
- Origin
- Raising

**Upper left: Black Angus**

**Upper right: Limousin**

**Center: Hereford**

**Lower left: Charolais**

**Lower right: Wagyu (Kobe)**

# Genetics

In our steak book everything revolves around beefsteaks. Cattle, as one of the oldest European domesticated animals, constitute a very essential component of human nutrition in the Western world. There are about 100 domesticated breeds of cattle. Most have only a regional importance; only a few breeds are known worldwide. The breeds are differentiated according to their uses: There are beef, milk, and two-use breeds. The best steaks come from the beef breeds.

**Well-known beef breeds are Black Angus, Hereford, Charolais, Limousin, and Simmental, plus the Japanese Wagyu. Since the Wagyu comes from the Kobe region, it is also known as Kobe beef.**

Because of their genetic qualities, there are some breeds that are best suited for beef use. Beef breeds offer advantages for both the farmer and the consumer—they have a very good value for their feed, meaning that they require less food than other breeds to build up muscles, and the proportion of muscles to the entire body is higher. Thus the gain per animal is higher for the farmer.

**The consumer's choice can be made completely according to personal preference.**

There are breeds that produce low-fat meat, such as the Charolais. But gourmets treasure strongly marbled beef, such as that of the Wagyu. Marbling refers to the fine veins of fat enclosed in the muscle, which melt during grilling and thus give the meat flavor, tenderness, and juiciness. Among those who know beef, the Black Angus and Hereford, along with the Wagyu, are the favorites because their meat shows high marbling regardless of their diet.

# Feeding

Genetics serve as the baseline, but how a beef producer raises and feeds beef breeds also determines the sensory criteria mentioned above: Taste, tenderness, and juiciness.

There are basically two methods of feeding used. One is feeding completely on grass, the other is feeding on so-called feed programs, in which other energy-rich foods are added.

In Europe and South America, grass feeding is almost always used. The USA and Japan, on the other hand, are known for their refined feeding programs. The more energy-rich the food is, the more easily the steer can build up intramuscular fat. But the flavor is also influenced by the feeding. We taste what the steers have eaten—in a positive but also a negative sense. Meat from animals that have enjoyed a purely grass diet is neutral in terms of taste because grass is not particularly flavor-intensive. But if the

steer eats grain or corn, then the meat has a much more intense flavor.

Along with the basic differences in the two feeding methods, efforts are made today to feed purely natural substances. The use of hormones has positive effects on the sensory quality, to be sure—the use of hormones means that more water is kept in the meat, so that it is juicier in principle—but we cannot say for sure today what effects eating this meat will have on our health. For this reason, the European lawmakers have banned the sale of hormone-treated meat in the European Union. On the other hand, the American lawmakers presently see the matter differently, and thus hormone-treated meat can be sold.

# Butchering Age

Cattle are mature in twelve months. The normal steer raised for the mass market is butchered at an age of 12 to 15 months. The steers of leading breeders, who supply the high-priced quality market for gourmets, on the other hand, are butchered at ages from 24 to 30 months. The renowned Wagyu steers are, as a rule, not butchered before the 36th month. But how does a different butchering age determine different quality?

The steer is in a growth phase until the twelfth month. It is not yet full-grown, and all the energy it takes in is devoted to growing. Only when the animal is full-grown, thus after the twelfth month, can ingested energy be devoted to building up fat reserves—intramuscular fat. The more time the steer has, the greater the marbling. Naturally, there is also an upper limit to the butchering age. If the animals get too old, the fibers are too tough, and the meat loses tenderness. In bison in particular, this effect can be seen clearly. Thus for high-quality meat, bisons are butchered only between the 24th and 30th month.

Before and during the butchering it must be assured that the animal is as stress-free as possible. The hormones built up by stress have a negative effect on the quality of the meat. Thus good breeders make sure that the animals are only transported a short distance before being butchered. If longer trips cannot be avoided, the animals should be given enough time to relax after being transported. As a rule this means one or two days.

# Aging

There are two reasons to age meat, especially beef. One is that the meat becomes tenderer during aging, and the other is that taste is further developed when the meet ages in air, also called aging on the bone.

There are two methods of aging meat. Today, aging in a vacuum is almost always used. Now and then meat is also aged in air. In the English-speaking world one speaks of wet-aging and dry-aging.

## Aging in a Vacuum

During aging in a vacuum, the individual pieces are made airtight in a vacuum and then stored at controlled temperatures.

The meat is made tenderer by the breaking of the albumin enzyme. Studies show that this process is finished after 28 days at 35°F (2°C). If the meat is eaten before the 28th day, it has not yet attained the tenderness that it could have. Aging beef more than 28 days has no effect on its tenderness. The controlled breakdown of the meat goes on until the point at which it is no longer fit to eat. As a rule, the producer marks a minimum usable date of three months on the meat, which is to be stored in its original vacuum packaging under maintained coldness. Since the aging depends very much on the temperature and contact with air, this date shortens very quickly if the meat is taken out of the vacuum or, for example, is stored at higher temperatures by retailers. Meat aged in vacuum is thus at its zenith when it has been cured optimally for about one month.

## Aging in Air / Aging on the Bone

Aging by the traditional method used before the vacuum process existed is more complicated.

Whole beef halves, or at least the choice cuts taken from the back, are cooled in controlled chambers or hung in the air. Today, this process, when it is practiced at all, is only done with the back area that contains the roast beef, fillet, and rib-eye.

First-class American steak houses that age rib-eye, T-bone, porterhouse, and New York strip in their own aging chambers usually prefer dry-aging. In comparison to aging in a vacuum, this process has several disadvantages for the producer, but the meat gourmet considers it a great advantage.

## Disadvantages

Larger cooling-room capacities are needed; meat aged in a vacuum can be stacked in boxes. This is not possible during the air-aging phase, since the air must circulate freely around the meat.

Depending on the humidity in the air of the aging chamber, the outer meat dries out and develops a mold at high humidity. This is a good kind of mold—the aroma in such a chamber is quite reminiscent of cheese mold—but before eating, and thus before selling, the dried-out and moldy meat has to be cut off or pared, which reduces the amount of meat. Only 50 to 70% of the original meat will be saleable. This is reflected in the sale price; only a small number of connoisseurs are ready to pay the higher price. Thus this process is not suitable for the mass market.

## The Advantage

For the meat lover, air-dried meat opens a whole new world of flavor. The meat takes on an intense flavor with a sweetish note. The optimal aging point is determined based on the desired intensity of the flavor, juiciness, and tenderness.

When meat is aged in air, two effects set in. One is that the flavor increases depending on the aging time, the other is that the meat loses juiciness; it dries out. The result is that the meat, the longer it ages, takes on a firmer bite. If one extended the aging over months and years, one would get an air-aged ham.

In the United States, where dry-aging is much more popular, the taste is most important. That means a firmer bite in a piece of meat is not regarded as a disadvantage. For the German, the tenderness of the meat is most important, and one would rather miss a bit of the flavor to have a tenderer, juicier steak.

The successful vendors of air-aged meat on the German and European market thus generally offer meat that has been aged 21 days. In the United States this time period can rise to as much as 56 days.

# Origin and Breeding

It is more and more important for the modern consumer to know where the foods that he consumes come from. This is particularly applicable to meat.

With the number of scandals about rotten or tainted meat, the existence of poor raising conditions, to which the animal-protection organizations and the Slow Food movement repeatedly call attention, this change in awareness is no surprise.

We human beings have eaten meat for tens of thousands of years, but more and more consumers have been sensitized by ethical considerations on the subject of proper animal treatment and avoidance of harm on the farm, in transit, and at the slaughterhouse. In this context in particular, the turn back to local products is more and more important. Pictures of large-scale cattle raising, often shown and denounced in the media, make clear that the consumer can influence which meat is offered for sale.

Only a very few consumers have the good fortune to have the best-quality beef offered to them right in their neighborhood. Except for Ireland, there is no notable cattle-raising nation in Europe that stands for very good meat quality. So in the future, too, it will be a fact that the meat gourmet, when he/she wants the best meat, will have to buy not regionally but globally. Thus we need a dealer or butcher whom we can trust, and who can show us that our concepts of origin and proper care are applied to the meat.

## Fresh or Frozen Meat?

Quality also means that the carefully produced meat reaches the steak lover in optimal condition. Through the development of the flash freezing process in recent years, there is an alternative to fresh meat. The Americans call this meat fresh-frozen: meat that was flash frozen to the optimal aging point for the purpose of sealing in the best quality of the meat. With beefsteak it can be assured that the consumer can eat it after the optimal curing time, which always depends on the aging process.

In the past, frozen meat was usually rated worse than fresh meat. This decision used to be justified, because the technique of freezing was insufficient. When products are frozen too long, large ice crystals form in their tissues and destroy the cells. Thus much fluid escapes during thawing, so that the meat quickly dries out during cooking. Then too, bacteria and germs can spread more quickly in the damaged cells.

In the flash-freezing process, the product freezes so fast that ice-crystal formation is limited to the extent that no quality is lost. The only factor to be observed is that the meat is thawed properly. This must be done slowly at a low temperature in the refrigerator. If the thawing is done too quickly, such as at room temperature, ice crystals form again, which damage the cells as previously mentioned.

**Today, one can observe the following development:** The probability that meat offered for sale has been flash-frozen becomes greater as the price becomes higher.

## Sources

**Nowadays, two sources offer their products to the steak lover:**

- **High-quality meat from the local region** can be bought from a trusted butcher. Hopefully, he can answer most questions about the criteria that are responsible for the quality of the meat. In many towns the regional breeder is also a source.

- **For internationally recognized top-quality meat,** there are now dealers who can send meat to the connoisseur and gourmet while guaranteeing that there are no breaks in the cold chain during transport. Just as with the choice of a regional source, one should naturally make sure in advance that the aforementioned criteria can be adhered to plausibly.

All quality naturally has its price, and the principle is that the higher the quality, the higher the price is. Since only a few consumers can—or want to—afford the best quality every day, the motto "less is more" or "I don't eat meat every day, but when I do, I afford good meat," can apply.

# Cuts

**All the pieces of meat that are suitable for grilling are classified as beefsteaks. The prerequisite for grilling is that the meat remains tender enough after a relatively short exposure to heat.**

Which cuts are to be considered depends on the quality of the meat. If the quality of the beef is especially bad, only the fillet is suitable. But if the meat quality is high and the meat is optimally aged, then pieces of it can be used as steak that would otherwise be intended for cooking or for grinding.

Thus it can be explained that in the United States, one of the leading meat-producing nations, many more cuts find their way onto the steak menu than in Germany. When one asks for a good steak in Germany, usually only fillet is offered.

Along with the tenderness and cut of a piece of meat that is suitable for use as a steak, flavor is naturally also an important criterion for making a choice. There are cuts that taste more intensively like steak than others. The intensity of the flavor depends on the marbling and from where on the animal the steak came from. Thus the entrecôte with the eye of fat tastes better than the fillet with little marbling, and the kidney from the interior of the abdomen has a stronger taste than roast beef.

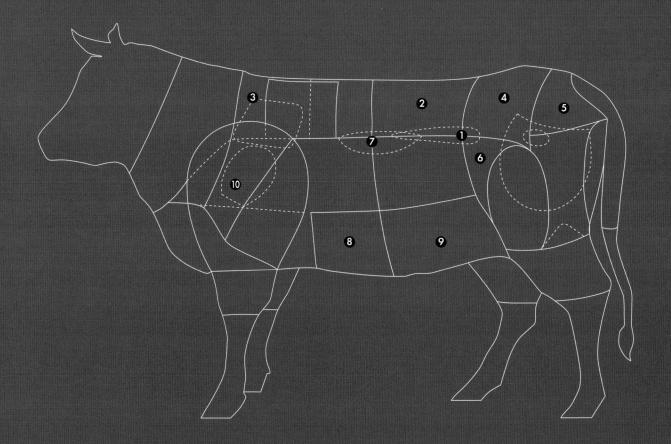

| 1 | Tenderloin | 6 | Tri-Tip steak | —— | outer pieces |
| 2 | T-bone and Porterhouse | 7 | Hanger steak | ------ | underlying pieces |
| 3 | Entrecôte (Ribeye, Delmonico) | 8 | Skirt steak | | |
| 4 | Sirloin | 9 | Flank steak | | |
| 5 | Rump cap (Sirloin cap) | 10 | Shoulder cut (Flatiron) | | |

Besides the quality of the meat itself, which determines the tenderness, the presentation of the steak can influence the perceived tenderness. There are cuts that are served as a whole steak, and those that are cut into pieces before serving. The latter are then easier to bite and are thus enjoyed as pleasantly tender, although they would fall on most diners' tenderness scale if they were served as a single piece.

Animals have muscles that are tenderer than others—the muscle used least often during the animal's life is tenderer. This knowledge has led some Japanese breeders of Kobe cattle to lift their animals slightly with slings, so that the muscles are used less often.

With proper breeding and tending, the largest muscles of cattle, which are naturally not used so much, are on the back. Entrecôte, roast beef, and interior fillets are exposed to considerably less stress than the shoulders, breast, and leg areas, which are constantly in use when the animal walks.

When buying steaks or carving them on your own, keep two things in mind to attain good cooking results:

• First, the steaks, if the final product allows, should be at least 3/4" (2 cm) thick. Thus the cooking time lasts longer than with thin-cut steak, but the chance that the meat reaches the desired aroma and optimal condition is considerably greater.

• Second, make sure that the steaks are cut with an equal thickness so they can cook evenly and the steak shows the desired condition at every point.

## The So-Called Premium Cuts and their Names

**When naming the cuts, one must be aware that there are often regional differences and variations. Here the most frequently used terms are cited.**

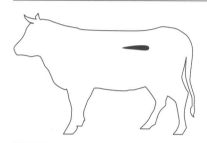

### Tenderloin

The tenderloin is the tenderest muscle. It is part of the back musculature but is scarcely flexed. The tenderloin is finely marbled and has a less intensive flavor. Medallions are cut from the fillet. Typical sizes are 4 1/4 oz, 5 2/3 oz, and 8 1/2 oz (120, 160 and 240 grams).

### Short-loin

The short loin is the rear part of the back muscle. It lies between the entrecôte and the rump. The steaks have an oval shape and are characterized by a coating of fat. Steaks from the short loin have a moderate flavor. Typical sizes are 9 oz, 10 1/2 oz, and 14 oz (250, 300, and 400 grams). In steak houses of the United States, short loin is cut into the New York strip steak or Kansas steak. With bone in, it is also called shell steak.

### Entrecôte/Ribeye/Delmonico

The entrecôte is the front part of the back muscle, bordering the striploin to the rear and the neck or tongue, as it is called in the trade, in front. The entrecôte has a nucleus of fat, also called a fat eye. Because of the high marbling, it is the most flavor-intensive of the premium cuts. It has an oval to round form. Typical steak sizes are 9 oz, 10 1/2 oz, and 14 oz (250, 300, and 400 grams). The entrecôte is also popularly prepared whole. It is also called the ribeye and the Delmonico. The ribeye with bone in is often called cowboy steak. The whole ribeye with bone in is called a ribeye roast and is a classic holiday roast.

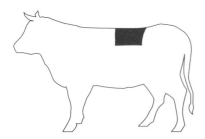

### T-Bone

The T-bone steak is so called because it has a T-shaped bone in the middle that differentiates the striploin from the tenderloin. The T-bone thus has two pieces of muscle: striploin and tenderloin. It has a small portion of tenderloin that is cut out of the flat part of the tenderloin or the fillet point. Typical T-bone sizes are 1 1/3 lb to 1 3/4 lb (600 to 800 grams).

### Porterhouse

The porterhouse is the T-bone's big brother. It is cut out of a part of the back in which the tenderloin has a larger diameter. Typical sizes are 1 2/3 lb to 2 lbs (750 to 900 grams). It is the classic steak of the American steak houses. It is usually aged in air in an aging chamber. The porterhouse name is in common use. In northern Italy it is called Bistecca alla Fiorentina.

## Other Well-known Steak Cuts:

### Sirloin

The sirloin is found in the rear quarter and adjoins the roast beef. The very thin cut consists of two muscles from the center of the hip and of the tenderer tenderloin of the hip. Oval steaks are cut from the center and medallions from the tenderloin. Although the cut is very thin, it has a more intense flavor than the tenderloin. Typical sizes are 7 oz to 10 1/2 oz (200 to 300 grams). The medallions are lighter, at 5 1/3 oz to 7 oz (150 to 200 grams). In the United States these cuts are called sirloin steaks or sirloin fillet steaks.

## The following cuts, at optimal meat quality, are also suitable for grilling:

### Sirloin Cap Steak

The sirloin cap steak is on the steak hip. This piece, weighing about 2 2/3 lb (1.2 kg), is called the Tafelspitz in Viennese cooking. In South America it is called Picanha. This tastily aged cut has a coating of fat. The muscle is less strongly marbled. Typical sizes for steaks cut from it are 7 oz to 10 1/2 oz (200 to 300 grams).

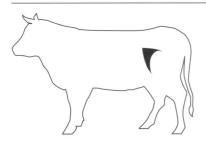

### Tri Tip

The "Mayor's Cut" is in the inner region of the hip. It is strongly marbled, very juicy, and tasty. Because of its flat triangular shape, steaks are cut as Pavets, which are rectangular long cuts with a typical weight of 3 oz to 4 1/4 oz (80 to 120 grams).

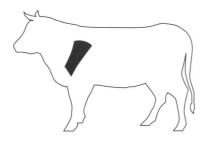

### Flat Iron

As an outstanding stew cut, it has long been called the flat iron steak in the United States. It consists of two muscles divided by a tendon. If it is divided there and the tendon is removed, one has two steaks in the shape of a flatiron; hence the "flat iron steak" name. Typical sizes are 5 1/3 oz to 9 oz (150 to 250 grams).

# The Kings of Flavor and Their Names

**The next three cuts are American specialties. They are grilled in the United States, while in Germany and Austria they are usually used as stewing or cooking meat.**

### Flank Steak

The flank steak is well-known in American steak houses. It is found in the rear part of the flank and is really too coarse-fibered for use as a steak cut. The thin flank steak is valued for its distinctive flavor, which can also take a marinade. The flank steak succeeds best when prepared medium rare and cut against the grain for serving. Another piece from this region is called the flap steak. Because of its flat, fanlike shape, it is usually cut into strips. The meat is strongly marbled and thus intensely flavored and juicy. In France it is called Bavette Aloyau.

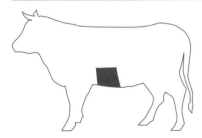

### Skirt Steak

The skirt steak helps hold the steer's belly together. It is a very strongly marbled thin steak. In Mexico it is the classic cut for fajitas. Like the flank steak, the skirt steak is very tasty and is usually marinated. It goes best when it is grilled medium rare and cut thin for serving.

### Hanging Steak

The hanging tenderloin lies in the chest cavity between the two kidneys. In American steak houses it is served as hanger steak. The most intensely flavored hanging tenderloin is prepared whole and cut into teardrops before serving. Typical weights are 14 oz to 1 1/3 lb (400 to 600 grams). Here, too, the best grilling is medium rare. The hanging tender loin is well known in France, where it is called Onglet.

# Preparation

Steaks should be tender and juicy and have a tasty sear with a roasting aroma.

Steaks are usually grilled so they taste better and become tenderer.

For this to happen, one should stick to the following procedure, regardless of which cut of steak it is.

**1.** Correct preparation of the steak

**2.** Creating roasting aromas and cooking

**3.** Resting the meat

## 1. Correct Preparation of the Steak

The correct preparation of a steak is not difficult, but following a few points is important to attain optimal results.

Take the steak out of the refrigerator at the right time so it can reach room temperature. Depending on how thick the steak is cut, it should be taken out of the refrigerator at least an hour before grilling. When the steak reaches room temperature, it can be grilled for a shorter time and thus more gently. Then too—and this is the more important aspect—the meat is more relaxed under the influence of heat. The result is a tenderer steak than meat that is cooked cold.

Dry the meat off well so the desired aromas can develop. Whether you salt it before or after grilling is purely a matter of taste and has no effect on the results. Those who refrain from salting first are correctly aware of the theoretical disadvantage that salt pulls water out of meat and the meat can thus become dry faster. In practice, this is scarcely provable.

## 2. Creating Roasting Aromas and Cooking

If one wants to prepare a really good steak, the roasting aromas are very important. The Maillard reaction is responsible for creating these aromas. In simple terms, it is a process in which, through the effect of dry heat, the sugars and proteins contained in the meat join and produce new materials which create a tasty brown sear. This reaction is found not only in steak, but in all roasting and baking processes in which a crust is formed, such as baking bread. This natural process is sometimes reinforced by cooks by strewing sugar on the meat before grilling. The dry heat must be over 248°F (120°C), at which point the Maillard reaction will always take place, whether one grills, roasts, or fries. American steak houses have perfected the creation of roasting aromas with high-performance gas ovens that heat up to 2190°F (1200°C). Anyone can decide how strongly their steak is to be roasted. In Germany the steak eater generally likes the crust a crisp brown, but not black. The Americans like it stronger and thus prefer a dark brown color with a touch of charring. As a process for attaining the extreme, the Americans use the so-called Pittsburgh style: black outside and raw inside.

# Cooking Temperatures

A cooking temperature is the point that meat attains a certain inner temperature and color. Generally, six finishing points are differentiated:

## very rare

The inner temperature is between 115°F and 124°F (46°C and 51°C).

The meat is red and has not changed from a raw state inside.

## rare

The inner temperature is between 124°F and 129°F (51°C and 54°C).

The meat is red and has not changed from a raw condition inside.

## medium rare

The inner temperature is between 129°F and140°F (54°C and 60°C).

The meat is a somewhat lighter red.

## medium

The inner temperature is between 140°F and 149°F (60°C and 65°C).

The meat is pink and the meat is half cooked.

## medium well

The inner temperature is between 149°F and 163°F (65°C and 73°C).

The meat is between pink and gray.

## well done

The inner temperature is between 165°F and 185°F (74°C and 85°C).

The meat is gray.

**Basically, the rule is:** The longer meat is grilled, the more liquid is withdrawn from it, and the more dry it becomes. If one wants juicy steak, it should be grilled to the medium level at most.

For very rare, rare, or even medium rare steaks, the idea that the steak is "bloody" has been accepted. This scares off many people. Who wants to eat something bloody? But the liquid that comes out, even with the wrong treatment, is not blood at all, but meat juice. Blood flows through vessels, and they are completely removed in butchering. The meat juice comes from the muscle cells. How one avoids letting the steak swim in its own blood when being cut, despite a "rare" temperature, will be explained in "Resting the Meat."

When preparing steaks it is good to work with two temperature zones. High heat to develop a brown sear (Maillard reaction), and low heat, ideally under 248°F (120°C), for cooking the steak to the desired cooking point.

With thicker steaks that take longer to reach temperature, a long time on high can result in burning the steak on the outside. By taking the steak off the grill when the desired roasting aromas are present, it can cook further without the Maillard effect.

This two-step procedure can run differently and also be done with different equipment. There is a difference between the so-called **forward cooking process** and the **backward cooking process**. In the forward process, the steak is first broiled and then finished over low heat. In the backward process, it is first brought to the desired inner temperature at low heat, and then the roasting aromas are attained over high heat.

## Classic Combinations of Equipment for the two Processes are:

**Pan and Oven:** Roasting aromas are attained in the pan. When this happens in the pan, use heat-resistant oil, clarified butter, or animal fat, thus fats that do not burn. The desired inner temperature is reached in the oven at a low temperature (such as 215°F [100°C]).

**One or Two Grills:** One can either control one grill so that one zone has a lower and one a higher temperature, or alternatively, work with two grills.

**Sous Vide and Pan or Grill:** The sous vide process has recently come into style. The steak is put in a vacuum-sealed bag and heated in an immersion circulator at a constant moderate temperature that equals the desired inner temperature. When that temperature is reached, one can add the roasting aromas to the steak in a pan or on a grill. The advantage of the sous vide process is that the meat reaches the inner temperature "stress-free" because the very small difference between room temperature and inner temperature is slowly bridged. This method is also "stress-free" for the cook. The steak can stay in the water bath for hours; because of the constant temperature of the water bath, the desired inner temperature cannot be exceeded.

## Methods of Determining Inner Temperature

The safest, but also most laborious, method is measuring the inner temperature with a **thermometer**. The process is safe because numbers simply do not lie. Of course this kind of measuring is also very demanding, for it cannot be carried out directly via the source of heat.

With even the best thermometers, to get an exact measurement one must make sure that it is inserted at several points in an area that is ten times the diameter of the needle. As a rule, this is only practicable when one inserts the thermometer from the side. Otherwise one must make sure that the measuring time always amounts to several seconds. This can be difficult with thin steaks that achieve roasting aromas and the desired inner temperature simultaneously. To attain the temperature, one must thus remove the meat from the heat. Naturally it is less problematic when the steaks are thicker and are prepared in the recommended two-stage process, since temperature measuring is then done in the lower temperature zone.

In spite of all that, the thermometer is the safest method, and thus it is recommended that one be on hand in the home. When buying, one should make sure that the insertion sensor is as thin as possible, so that the hole it makes remains as unnoticeable as possible. You don't have to stick it in too far to get an exact measurement.

Whoever has the time to practice can try the **finger-pressing method**. Here you press your index finger on the middle of the steak. The firmer the meat feels, the further along in the cooking process it is. Raw meat feels soft and gives way without pressure. This indicates the rare stage. As soon as you feel a trace of change from the soft condition, the meat goes into the medium rare stage. If the meat gives way but springs back lightly, it is medium. If it moves back slowly, it is medium well. If it feels firm and does not move, it is well done.

Another method shows when the steak is medium rare. With a normal steak thickness of 3/4" (2 cm), the steak is grilled about four minutes on one side. If it is then turned, look closely at the already-grilled upper side of the steak, If meat juice is dripping out, then the steak is medium rare.

**The question of how often one should turn a steak is easily answered: It should be turned only once to achieve even grilling results. Frequent turning just lengthens the grilling time needlessly.**

**When measuring the cooking point, remember that the steak still must rest, and that the inner temperature can rise several degrees depending on the thickness of the steak.**

# 3. Resting the Meat

Like any meat, a steak consists mainly of liquid. Through heating, the liquid is pushed away from the heat into the center of the meat. This increases pressure that is released when the meat is cut. The pressure can become so strong that the meat juice really squirts out of the steak, for example, when one sticks a fork into it, which one should not do. Instead, it is better to move or turn the meat with tongs.

To avoid this, the meat should rest before being cut. Resting means that the meat should be kept warm for several minutes before it is cut. In this time the previously compressed meat juice spreads evenly in the steak. The pressure decreases and the juice is again where it was before. If the steak is cut at this point, ideally no meat juice runs out. The longer the meat can stand, the less juice comes out while cutting.

To keep it warm while standing, one must make sure that the steak does not cook further. Thus the temperature must be under the desired cooking point. On the other hand, the surroundings should be warm enough so that the meat does not cool off.

A simple method is wrapping the meat in aluminum foil, which isolates the meat and does not let it cool off. If one later serves the steaks on pre-warmed plates, one prevents the steak from cooling too fast, and large steaks stay warm longer.

# RECIPES

All recipes are planned
for four people

Prepared in
the pan

ENTRECÔTE

RIBEYE

DELMONICO

# Mini-Salami Ribeye

| | |
|---|---|
| 2 1/4 lbs (1000 g) | **Ribeye in one piece** |
| 4 | **Mini-salamis** |
| 1/2 lb (200 g) | **Gouda cheese in one piece** |
| 1 bunch | **Spring onions** |
| 2 Tbsp | **Paprika** |
| 1 Tbsp | **Salt** |
| 1 tsp | **Cumin** |
| 1 Tbsp | **Brown sugar** |
| 1 tsp | **Garlic powder** |
| 1 tsp | **Cayenne pepper** |

Cut the cheese into four equally large pieces. Wash the spring onions and cut to the length of the steak. With a pointed knife, make 12 holes through the steak. Stick a mini-salami, strip of cheese, or onion alternately into the holes. Mix the spices well, rub them onto the steak, and let it set in the refrigerator for six hours. Grill the steak on the hot grill, turning often, to an inner temperature of 133°F (56°C). Let it stand a bit and then cut it into four equally large pieces.

**Suggested sides:**

Colorful salad, depending on season and taste.

 One can also fry this steak in as heavy a cast iron pan as possible until an inner temperature of 133°F (56°C) is reached.

# Ribeye
# Surf & Turf
# with Scallops

4   **Ribeye steaks, 1 1/8" (3 cm) thick**

4   **Scallops**

    **Zest and juice of one lemon**

    **Salt**

    **Pepper**

    **Sugar**

Season the steaks with salt, pepper, and some sugar and grill four minutes on each side. Drip lemon juice on the scallops and season with salt, pepper, and sugar. Broil the scallops on a cast plate for a maximum of half a minute on each side. Cut out the fat eye of each steak and stick a scallop into the steak. Strew the lemon zest over it and serve.

**Suggested sides:**

Grilled vegetables, see page 128

 Cook the steaks in a pan one minute longer than the grill time, but broil the scallops for only half a minute per side so they remain glassy.

# Ribeye
# Japanese Style

| | |
|---|---|
| 4 | **Ribeye steaks, 1/2 lb (250 g) each** |
| 6 Tbsp | **Soy sauce** |
| 3/8 cup (100 ml) | **Dry white wine** |
| 3/8 cup (100 ml) | **Sherry** |
| 1 Tbsp | **White balsamic vinegar** |
| 2 tsp | **Honey** |
| 1/2 tsp | **Ground allspice** |
| 1 tsp | **Ginger powder** |
| 1 tsp | **Ground black pepper** |
| 1 tsp | **Salt** |

Mix all the ingredients for the marinade well and marinate the steaks in it in the refrigerator for 12 hours. Take the steaks out of the marinade, let them drip dry, and fry them in a hot pan for three to four minutes on each side. Let them stand briefly, and then serve.

**Suggested sides:**
Grilled artichokes, see page 132

# Ribeye
# Cooked Backward

| | |
|---|---|
| 2 1/4 lbs (1000 g) | **Ribeye in one piece** |
| 1 Tbsp | **Onion powder** |
| 1 Tbsp | **Garlic powder** |
| 1 tsp | **Salt** |
| 2 tsp | **Ground black pepper** |
| 1 tsp | **Smoked paprika powder** |

Rub the ribeye with the spices and put it in the oven for 45 minutes at 275°F (140°C). Then take it out and cut it into four equally large pieces. Fry the four pieces in the pan again for 1 1/2 minutes on each side over high heat.

**Suggested sides:**

Sliced potatoes with herb sour cream, see page 130

# Ribeye
# Stirred not Shaken

| | |
|---|---|
| 4 | Ribeye steaks, 1/2 lb (250 g) each |
| 3 | Garlic cloves |
| 5 Tbsp | Gin |
| 5 Tbsp | Vermouth |
| 4 Tbsp | Canola oil |
| 1 tsp | Salt |
| 1 tsp | Ground black pepper |
| 1 Tbsp | Chopped basil |
| 1 tsp | Fresh chopped oregano |
| | Olives filled with pimento |

Peel the garlic and dice. Put the gin and vermouth into a bowl. Add oil, salt, pepper, basil, and oregano and stir well.

Marinate the ribeye steaks in it for two hours. Let the meat drip dry and grill four minutes on each side. Let them stand briefly, stick the olives on wooden skewers and serve with the steaks.

**Suggested sides:**
Ciabatta with homemade herb butter

In a pan, add 1 min. per side to the grill time.

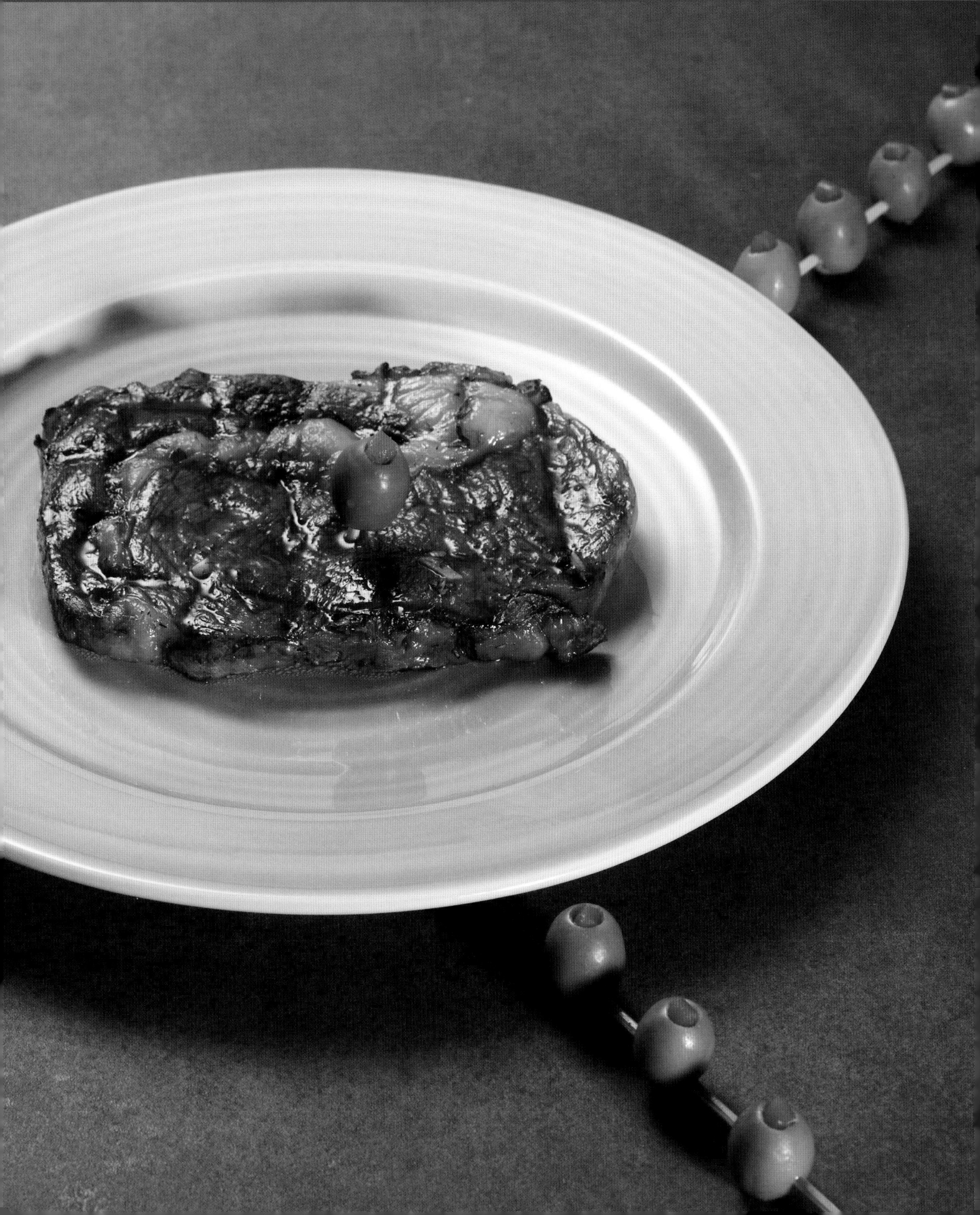

# Delmonico
# from the Kingdom

| | |
|---|---|
| 1 3/4 lb (800 g) | **Delmonico** |
| 4 | **Tomatoes** |
| 4 | **Slices bacon** |
| 8 Tbsp | **Canola oil** |
| 3 Tbsp | **Dijon mustard** |
| 1 Tbsp | **Ground black pepper** |
| | **Coarse sea salt** |

Stir the canola oil with the mustard and pepper and coat the Delmonico with it. Grill the meat on all four sides for four minutes per side at high heat.

Cut crosswise into the tomatoes, cover each with a strip of bacon, and add to the meat on the grill for the last five minutes. Let the meat stand briefly after grilling, then cut four equally large pieces, sprinkle the salt on it, and serve with the tomatoes.

**Suggested sides:**

Rosemary potatoes

In a pan, add 1 min. per side to the grill time.

# Delmonico Coburg Style

| | |
|---|---|
| 4 | **Slices Delmonico, ca. 1/2 lb (200 g) each** |
| 5 | **Red onions** |
| 3 | **Garlic cloves** |
| 4 Tbsp | **Canola oil** |
| | **Ground black pepper** |
| | **Salt** |

Peel the onions and cut into thin rings. Peel the garlic cloves and cut into thin strips. Put two tablespoons of canola oil into a bowl, put two slices of meat on it, season with salt and pepper, and cover with half the onions and garlic. Put the other two slices of meat on, season, and cover with the other half of the onions and garlic. Cover the bowl and put in the refrigerator for six hours.

Prepare the grill for direct grilling and grill the steaks four to five minutes on each side.

**Suggested sides:**
Scamorza potatoes, see page 126

In a pan, add 1 min. per side to the grill time.

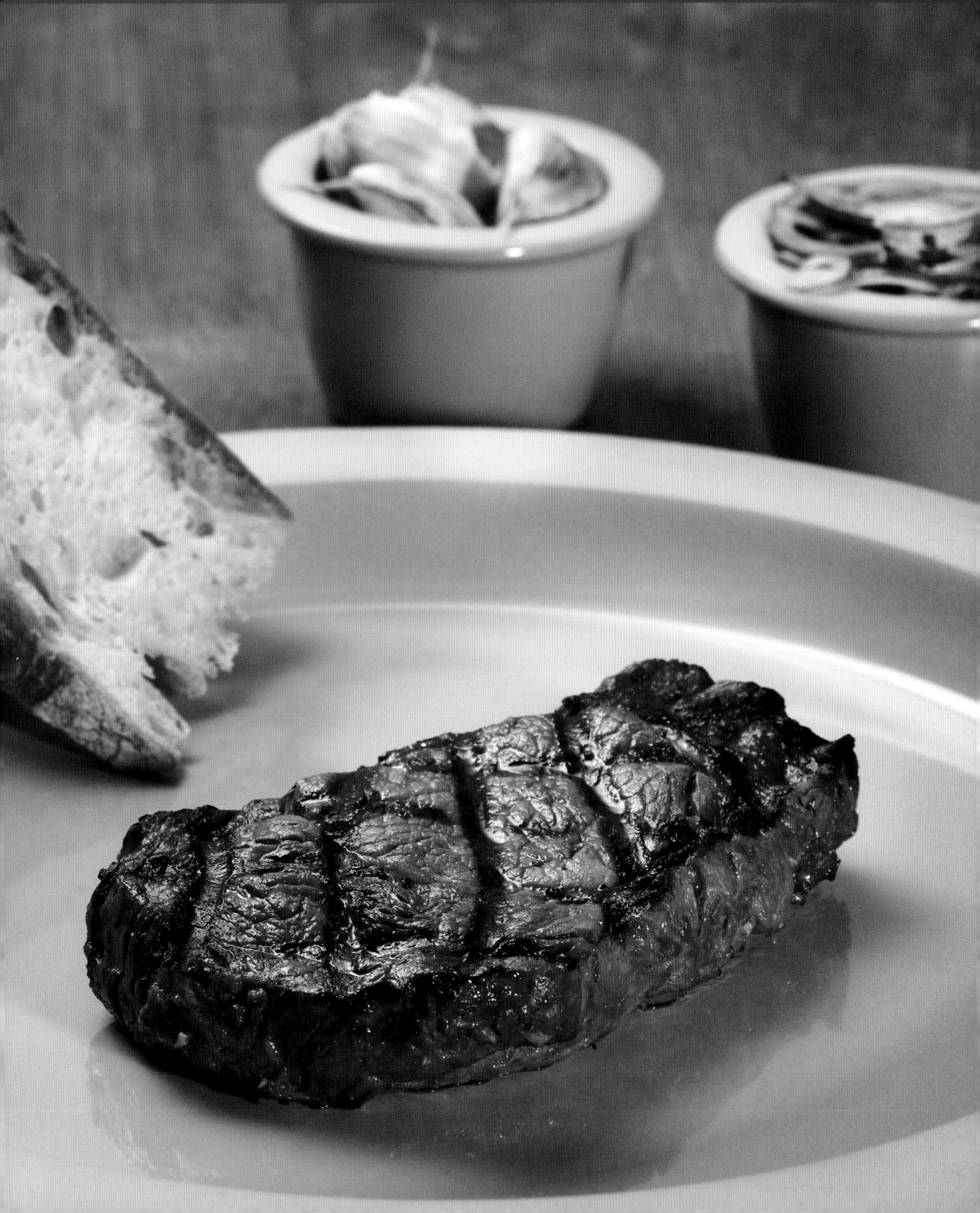

# TENDERLOIN

# Tenderloin on Fire

| | |
|---|---|
| 1 3/4 lb – 2 1/4 lbs (800–1000 g) | **Beef tenderloin in one piece** |
| 2 | **Onions** |
| 1 | **Ginger root, ca. 1 1/2 " (4 cm)** |
| 5 | **Garlic cloves** |
| 4 | **Scotch Bonnet or Habanero chili peppers, without seeds** |
| 2 cups (500 ml) | **Grapefruit juice** |
| 1/4 cup (60 ml) | **Soy sauce** |
| 1/4 cup (60 ml) | **Walnut oil** |
| 1 tsp | **Crushed black pepper** |

Remove tendons and fat from the beef fillet. Peel the onions, ginger, and garlic and chop them fine. Remove the seeds from the chili peppers and chop them fine. Pour the grapefruit juice, walnut oil, and soy sauce into a bowl and add the onions, ginger, garlic, and chili peppers. Mix it all well, put the beef fillet in the bowl and cover with marinade. Marinate in the refrigerator for at least 12 hours. Take the fillet out of the marinade, pat dry, and grill on all sides to an inner temperature of 130°F (54°C), or fry in a pan, then wrap in aluminum foil and let it stand for five minutes. Cut even medallions for serving. You can reduce the number of chili peppers if you are cooking for someone who doesn't like spicy food.

**Suggested sides:**
Grilled vegetables, see page 128

# Tenderloin
# Meets Beef Brisket

| | |
|---|---|
| 4 | **Tenderloin steaks, ca. 1/2 lb (200 g) each** |
| 1 lb (400 g) | **Beef brisket** |
| 1 | **Leek stalk** |
| 1 | **Large carrot** |
| 1 | **Onion** |
| 1/4 | **Celery stalk** |
| 1 Tbsp | **Salt** |

**STEFAN MARQUARD:**

"Here beef brisket is finally set in the right scene."

Peel the carrot, onion, leek, and celery stalk and chop coarsely. Put it all in a pot with 8 1/2 cups (2 l) of water and one tablespoon salt, and bring to a boil. Reduce the temperature so that it just barely boils. Put the beef brisket in the water and cook covered for an hour. The water must not boil any more. Meanwhile, cut a cross about 1" (2.5 cm) wide in the middle of each fillet with a knife. Cut the cooked beef brisket into four equal slices 1" (2.5 cm) wide and stick them into the fillet. Trim off the excess brisket. Season the fillets with salt, pepper, and some sugar and grill each side for three minutes over high heat.

**Suggested sides:**

Potatoes with herb sour cream, see page 130

In a pan, add 1 min. per side to the grill time.

# Filet Mignon

| | |
|---|---|
| 4 | **Filet Mignon, ca. 5 2/3 oz (160 g ) each** |
| 4 | **Slices bacon** |
| Some | **Sea salt** |
| Several | **Black peppercorns, crushed crudely** |
| Some | **Sugar** |

Season the filet mignon with sea salt, pepper, and some sugar. Then wrap the bacon around them, fasten it with a toothpick, and grill each side two minutes on a hot grill. Let it stand briefly before serving. Filet Mignon is the classic kind of steak.

**Suggested sides:**

Arugula salad with Parmesan sticks

In a pan, add 1 min. per side to the grill time.

# Pickled Tenderloin

| Ca. 1 3/4 lb (800 g) | Middle steak from beef tenderloin |
| --- | --- |
| 4 cups (1 liter) | Dry red wine |
| 3/8 cup (100 ml) | Red wine vinegar |
| 1 | Onion |
| 1/2 bunch | Mustard greens |
| 5 | Juniper berries |
| 1 | Bay leaf |
| | Salt |
| | Pepper |

Dice the onion and chop the mustard greens finely. Pour the wine and vinegar into a bowl, add the juniper berries, bay leaf, onion, and mustard greens, put the steak in, and marinate 24 hours.

Take the meat out the next day, pat dry, and cut medallions 1 1/2" (4 cm) thick from it. Fry three minutes on each side in a pan over high heat.

**Suggested sides:**

Grilled artichokes, see page 132

STEFAN MARQUARD:

"Who says you can't pickle a roast? It works great with brief frying, too."

# Sicilian Tenderloin Steak

| | |
|---|---|
| 4 | Tenderloin steaks, each ca. 1/2 lb (200 g) |
| 12 | Anchovy fillets in oil from a jar |
| 2 Tbsp | Olive oil |
| 2 Tbsp | Tarragon vinegar |
| 2 Tbsp | Dry sherry |
| 3 | Garlic cloves, pressed |
| 1/2 Tbsp | Fresh oregano leaves, chopped |
| 1/2 Tbsp | Fresh tarragon leaves, chopped |
| | Black pepper |
| | Sea salt |

Crush the anchovies with a fork and put in a bowl with the olive oil, tarragon vinegar, garlic, and sherry. Mix in the spices and marinate the steaks in them for an hour.

Take the steaks out of the marinade and grill each side for three minutes. Take from the grill, sprinkle with black pepper and sea salt, and serve with the remaining marinade.

**Suggested sides:**
Grilled vegetables, see page 128

In a pan, add 1 min. per side to the grill time.

# Tenderloin Steak Stuffed with Cannelloni

| | |
|---|---|
| 4 | **Tenderloin steaks, each ca. 1/2 lb (200 g)** |
| 8 | **Cannelloni** |
| 8 | **Bacon slices** |
| 1/2 lb (200 g) | **Spinach** |
| 2 | **Red chili peppers** |
| 2 | **Garlic cloves** |
| 2 Tbsp | **Sesame seeds** |
| | **Olive oil** |
| | **Salt & Pepper** |

Cut two longitudinal slits in each steak with a carving knife and widen them with a cooking spoon so the cannelloni can be pushed in. Cook the cannelloni four minutes in a pot of salted water; they must still be firm.

For the filling, wash the spinach and let drip dry. Remove the seeds from the peppers and chop small, dice the garlic cloves. Heat some olive oil in a pan, sauté the garlic and peppers five minutes, add the sesame seeds after three minutes, and brown them. Mix the spinach with the garlic, peppers, and sesame; fill the cannelloni with them. Insert the filled cannelloni into the steaks and trim the excess from the ends. Wrap each steak with two strips of bacon, fasten with a toothpick, season with salt and pepper, and grill on each side for three minutes. Then let stand five minutes at 140°F (60°C) and serve.

**Suggested sides:**

Colorful salad with olives

In a pan, add 1 min. per side to the grill time.

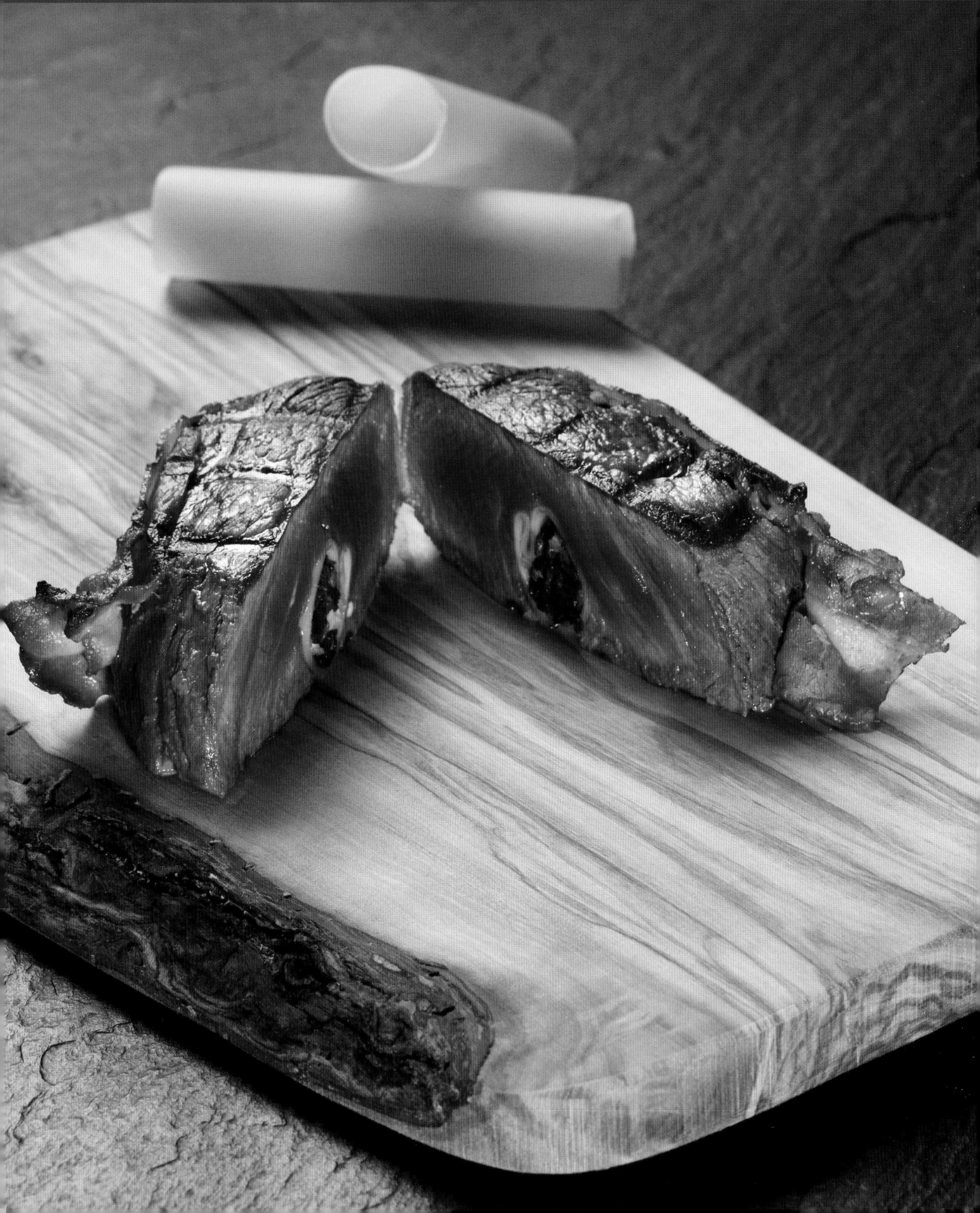

# Tenderloin
# Steak Tartare

| | |
|---|---|
| 4 | Tenderloin medallions, each ca. 5 2/3 oz (160 g) |
| | Juice of one lime |
| | Juice of one lemon |
| | Salt |
| | Pepper |
| | Sugar |
| 6 | Basil leaves |
| 1/4 lb (100 g) | Arugula |
| 1 | Block Parmesan cheese |

On one side of the steak cut several times downward to the middle of the steak to create a pattern of cubes about 1/8" (3 mm) square. Pour the lime and lemon juice into a bowl, chop the basil leaves fine, add them, and season with salt, pepper, and some sugar. Keep cool. Season the steaks with salt, pepper, and sugar and fry three minutes on the uncut side. If you use a grilling pan or grill, you can also turn the steaks 90 degrees for a minute and a half, getting a nice grill pattern.

Arrange the arugula on the plates, put the steaks on with the cubed side up, pour the sauce over them and shave some Parmesan on top.

**Suggested sides:**
Ciabatta with homemade herb butter

# Tenderloin in Sesame Coating

| | |
|---|---|
| 4 | **Tenderloin steaks, 1/2 lb (200 g) each** |
| 1/2 cup (125 ml) | **Soy sauce** |
| 4 Tbsp | **Flour** |
| 2 | **Eggs** |
| 4 Tbsp | **Sesame** |
| 3 Tbsp | **Canola oil** |
| | **Salt** |
| | **Pepper** |

Marinate the steaks in the soy sauce for two hours. Brown the sesame in a small pan. Pat the steaks dry and season with salt and pepper. Beat the eggs on a plate, dredge the steaks in flour, egg, and sesame, and fry each side for three minutes in canola oil in a pan over high heat. Let stand for five minutes and then serve.

**Suggested sides:**

Tomato grapefruit mango salsa, see page 129

# Onion Steak

| | |
|---|---|
| 4 | Tenderloin steaks, ca. 1/2 lb (200 g) each |
| 3 | Medium onions |
| 2 Tbsp | Canola oil |
| | Salt |
| | Pepper |
| | Sugar |

Season the steaks with salt, pepper, and some sugar. Heat the canola oil in the pan and brown the steaks on high heat for two minutes on each side.

Take the steaks out of the pan and let rest in aluminum foil for five minutes in the oven. Cut the onions into thin rings and fry golden brown in the pan juice. Put the steaks on plates and garnish with the onions.

**Suggested sides:**
Grilled vegetables, see page 128

# SIRLOIN STEAK

# Colorful Mixed Grill

| | |
|---|---|
| 4 | Sirloin steaks, 1/2 lb (200 g) each |
| 4 | Lamb cutlets |
| 1 lb (400 g) | German sausage without casing |
| 4 | Chicken drumsticks |
| 8 Tbsp | Canola oil |
| 2 Tbsp | Red wine vinegar |
| 4 | Garlic cloves |
| 1 tsp | Salt |
| 1 tsp | Pepper |
| 1 tsp | Paprika powder |

Peel the garlic and press it through a press. Mix the oil, vinegar, and pressed garlic with the spices. Brush the steaks, cutlets, sausage and chicken with the marinade.

Grill the chicken drumsticks seven minutes on each side, the steaks four minutes on each side, the lamb cutlets and sausage three minutes on each side.

After turning them, brush them all with marinade again. Put one piece of each meat on each plate.

**Suggested sides:**
Grilled vegetables, see page 128

# Sirloin Sandwiches with Fennel

| | |
|---|---|
| 4 | Sirloin steaks, ca. 1/2 lb (200 g) each |
| 4 | Pita bread pieces |
| 1 | Handful of arugula |
| 1 | Fennel bulb, sliced thin |
| 1 | Red onion, sliced thin |
| 1 | Garlic clove, pressed |
| 1 Tbsp | Coarse Dijon mustard |
| 2 Tbsp | White wine vinegar |
| 4 tsp | Fine sugar |
| | Salt |
| | Pepper |
| | Olive oil |

Heat the olive oil in a pan, add the fennel, onion, and garlic, and simmer lightly. Raise the temperature, add the sugar, and caramelize, stirring constantly, until everything slowly browns. Stir in the mustard and vinegar and season with salt and pepper. Cook ten minutes and stir again.

Grill the steaks four minutes on each side. Cut the pita bread in the middle and grill each piece one minute. Spread the fennel-onion mixture on the lower part of the pita, put a steak on it, season with salt and pepper, put the arugula on top of it, and cover with the upper half of the bread.

In a pan, add 1 min. per side to the grill time.

# Florentine Sirloin Steak

| | |
|---|---|
| 4 | Sirloin steaks, ca. 1/2lb (200 g ) each |
| 4 | Thin slices of hot smoked porkbelly |
| 10 | Bacon slices |
| 8 | Sage leaves |
| 8 | Olives filled with pimento |
| | Olive oil |
| 2 Tbsp | Roasted sesame seeds |
| | Salt |
| | Pepper |

Season the steaks with salt and pepper. Strew with sesame seeds. Put a slice of smoked porkbelly on each steak. Halve the olives, put four olive halves and two sage leaves on each steak, and wrap with bacon. Brush with olive oil and grill five minutes on each side.

**Suggested sides:**

Scamorza potatoes, see page 126

 In a pan, add 1 min. per side to the grill time.

# Octopus & Steak
# Surf & Turf

| | |
|---|---|
| 4 | **Sirloin steaks, ca. 1/2 lb (200 g) each** |
| 20 | **Octopus legs** |
| 2-3 | **Onions, quartered** |
| 1 | **Garlic bulb, the individual cloves peeled and halved** |
| 1/2 | **Bunch chives** |
| | **Salt** |
| | **Pepper** |

Let the octopus simmer for 30 minutes at low heat in salt water with the onions and garlic. Cut the chives into small tubes. Season the sirloin on both sides with salt and pepper. Cut five holes into each steak and sear on one side for two minutes. Remove the steak from the pan and pull the octopus legs through the beef. Make sure the raw side is on the bottom, the side the octopus legs are not sticking out of.

Fry the raw side two minutes and put the steaks into a preheated oven for another 15 minutes at ca. 160°F (70°C) until finished.

Place on pre-warmed plates and scatter the chives over them.

**Suggested sides:**
Grilled artichokes, see page 132

STEFAN MARQUARD:

"This is not only an eye-catcher, but it also tastes sensational."

78

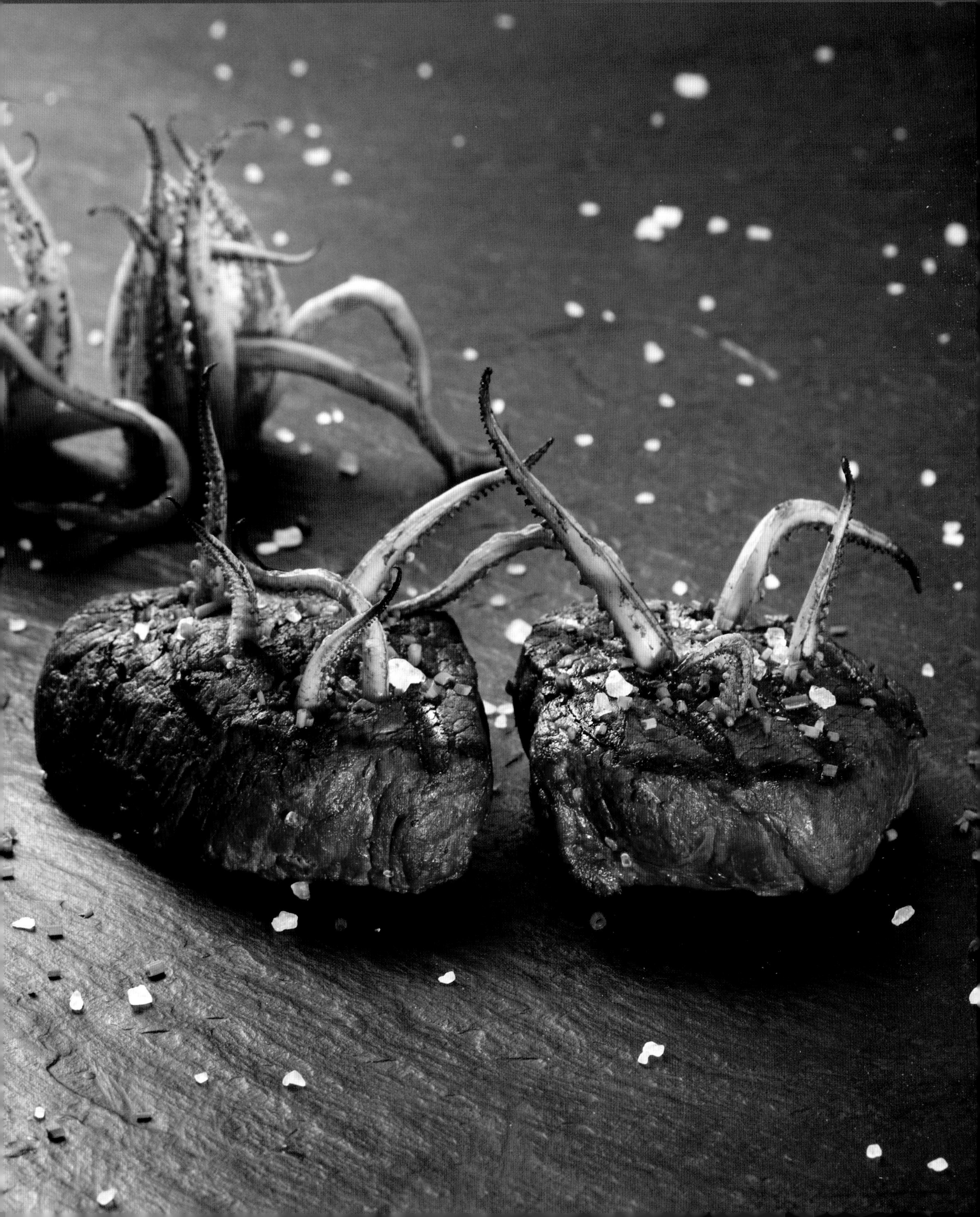

# RUMP STEAK

# Garlic Rump Steak

| | |
|---|---|
| 4 | **Rump steaks, ca. 1/2 lb (200 g) each** |
| 1 | **Fresh garlic bulb** |
| 2 Tbsp | **Olive oil** |
| 1/4 lb (100 g) | **Butter, at room temperature** |
| 1 Tbsp | **Fresh thyme** |
| 1 Tbsp | **Fresh rosemary** |
| | **Salt** |
| | **Pepper** |
| | **Sugar** |

Wrap the garlic, skin and all, and the olive oil in aluminum foil and let it cook ca. 40 minutes in the oven at 320°F (160°C). When the garlic is soft, press it out of its skin and put it in the mixer with the butter, thyme, and rosemary; mix to a smooth cream. Season with salt and pepper. Season the steaks with salt, pepper, and some sugar and fry three minutes on each side. Arrange the steaks on the plates, coat with the garlic butter, and serve at once.

**Suggested sides:**

Colorful salad with garlic croutons

# Rump Steak from the Herb Garden

| | |
|---|---|
| 4 | Rump steaks, 1/2 lb (200 g) each |
| 1 Tbsp | Watercress |
| 1 Tbsp | Basil |
| 1 Tbsp | Thyme |
| 1 Tbsp | Tarragon leaves |
| 1 Tbsp | Chives |
| 2 | Shallots |
| 2 | Garlic cloves |
| 1 tsp | Fresh horseradish |
| | Salt |
| | Pepper |
| 4 Tbsp | Olive oil |
| 4 Tbsp | Calvados |
| 2 Tbsp | Dry sherry |

Put all of ingredients (except the steaks) in a mixer and mix until a smooth, flowing cream results. Lay the steaks in the marinade and leave them in the refrigerator for four hours. Then take them out, pat dry, and grill three minutes on each side. Season with salt and pepper before serving.

**Suggested sides:**

Potatoes with herb sour cream, see page 130

In a pan, add 1 min. per side to the grill time.

# Caribbean Rump Steak

| 4 | Rump steaks, 1/2 lb (200 g) each |
|---|---|
| 1 | Fresh pineapple |
| 2 | Garlic cloves |
| 1 tsp | Coriander |
| 1 tsp | Cayenne pepper |
| 4 Tbsp | Canola oil |

Peel the pineapple, remove the core, and cut into cubes. Peel the garlic, put in the mixer with the pineapple and coriander, and mix to a smooth cream. Then add the cayenne pepper. Marinate the steaks in it for at least six hours. Take the meat out of the marinade, pat dry, and grill three minutes on each side.

**Suggested sides:**

Tomato grapefruit mango salsa, see page 129

In a pan, add 1 min. per side to the grill time.

# Swiss Rösti Rump Steak

| 4 | Rump steaks, ca. 1/2 lb (200 g each) |
| 1 1/8 lb (500 g) | Baking potatoes |
| 1/2 | Onion |
| 1/4 tsp | Salt |
| 1 Tbsp | Canola oil |
| 1 Tbsp (15 g) | Butter |

Wash the potatoes thoroughly and put in a pot with boiling salted water. They should be well covered by the water. Cook ten minutes in rapidly boiling water, then drain, cool, and peel. Then grate on a grater with teardrop-shaped holes. Peel the onion, chop very finely, and mix with the potatoes and salt. Brown the steaks in a hot pan for one minute on each side.

Take the steaks out of the pan and dredge it in the grated potato mixture. Fry the coated steaks in the pan on each side until a nice brown crust forms.

**Suggested sides:**
Colorful salad—depending on season and taste

# Pepper Steak

| | |
|---|---|
| 4 | **Rump steaks** |
| 2 Tbsp | **Canola oil** |
| 1 Tbsp | **Tomato paste** |
| 2 Tbsp | **Green peppercorns** |
| 2 Tbsp | **Sherry** |
| 1 cup (250 ml) | **Cream** |
| | **Salt** |
| | **Pepper** |

Heat the oil in a pan, brown the steaks on high heat for two minutes on each side. Preheat the oven to 175°F (80°C) and wrap the steaks in aluminum foil after browning and put them in the oven. Put the tomato paste in the pan with the pan juice and heat somewhat, then pour in the sherry. Add the cream and peppercorns and season with salt and pepper. Arrange the steaks on the plates and serve with the sauce. All kinds of potatoes are a good accompaniment for this steak dish.

**Suggested sides:**

Scamorza potatoes, see page 126

# Roast Beef
# in a Black Coat

| | |
|---|---|
| 4 | Roast beef steaks, ca. 1/2 lb (200 g) each |
| 4 Tbsp | Soy sauce |
| 2 Tbsp | Black sesame |
| 1 | Small ginger root, ca. 3/4" (2 cm) |
| 2 | Garlic cloves |
| 2 | Thai chili peppers |
| 1 Tbsp | Sea salt |
| 1 tsp | Ground black pepper |
| | Canola oil |
| | Butter |

Peel the garlic and ginger and chop finely; remove seeds from peppers and cut small. Pour the soy sauce into a bowl, add all other ingredients, except the meat, and stir thoroughly. Coat the steaks with it on both sides and marinate over-night. Heat the canola oil and butter in a pan. Fry the steaks four minutes on each side over medium heat. Take the pan off the heat and let the steaks stand for five minutes.

Suggested sides:
Devil's corn, see page 131

# Roast Beef Steakburger

| | | | | | | |
|---|---|---|---|---|---|---|
| 1 3/4 lb (800 g) | **Roast beef** | 2 | | **Small zucchini** | | **Salt** |
| 1 | **Eggplant** | 2 | | **Garlic cloves** | | **Pepper** |
| 1 | **Red onion** | 2 Tbsp | | **Olive oil** | | **Sugar** |
| 2 | **Red peppers** | 2 | | **Tomatoes** | | |

Cut the roast beef into eight thin slices. Wash the eggplant and zucchini, cut them into eight thin slices each. Cut the onion into fine rings, quarter the pepper, remove the seeds, peel the tomatoes and remove their seeds. Brush the vegetables with olive oil and lay them on the hot grill: Peppers ten minutes; tomatoes eight; onion rings, zucchini, and eggplant about four minutes—turn after half the time. The pepper's charred skin can now be removed easily. Press the garlic cloves, put in a bowl with the peppers and tomatoes, and mix with a hand mixer. Season with salt, pepper, and sugar. Season the roast beef slices with salt and pepper and brown on one side.

**Now lay a slice of roast beef on its ungrilled side and build up the "burger filling" as follows:**
One slice zucchini, one slice eggplant, and finally one slice of roast beef with the grilled side on the eggplant, so that the raw side is outside. Pin the burger with a wooden skewer and grill four minutes on each side.

 Preheat the oven to 475°F (250°C). Put the pepper quarters on a sheet with the skin side up and leave in the oven until the skin turns black and forms bubbles. Put the peppers in a bowl, let cool briefly and then remove the skin. Put the tomatoes in a bowl, pour boiling water over them, and skin them. Then chop them coarse and brown strongly in the pan until they are very soft. Then prepare them along with the peppers as described above.

In a pan, grill the pinned burgers about one minute longer on each side than the grilling time.

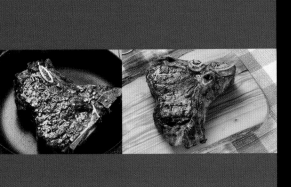

# T-BONE

# PORTERHOUSE

# Stuffed T-Bone Steak

| | |
|---|---|
| 2 | T-bone steaks, ca. 1 1/8" (3 cm) thick |
| 1/4 lb (100 g) | Gouda cheese, grated |
| 2 | Tarragon sprigs, chopped small |
| 2 Tbsp | Dijon mustard |
| | Salt |
| | Pepper |
| | Oregano leaves |

Cut a small pocket in each T-bone steak with a sharp knife.

Mix the Gouda, tarragon, oregano leaves, and Dijon mustard and press into the pocket. You can close the pockets with toothpicks, but it is more classy to stick a champagne cork into the opening. Season the steaks with pepper and salt and fry eight minutes on each side in a hot pan. Let stand briefly and then serve.

**Suggested sides:**
Devil's corn, see page 131

**STEFAN MARQUARD:**

"Now there is finally another use for the champagne cork."

98

# Classic T-Bone

| | |
|---|---|
| 4 | T-bone steaks, ca. 1 1/8" (3 cm) thick |
| 4 Tbsp | Garlic powder |
| 4 Tbsp | Onion powder |
| 2 Tbsp | Black pepper, ground |
| 2 tsp | Salt |
| 1 Tbsp | Rose paprika |
| 1 Tbsp | Brown sugar |
| 4 Tbsp | Canola oil |

Mix the spices well, rub them on both sides of the T-bone steaks, and marinate for at least two hours. Heat the canola oil on high heat in two pans (steak pans are best) and fry the steaks five minutes on each side. Take them out of the pans and let stand five minutes in aluminum foil.

**Suggested sides:**

Potatoes with herb sour cream, see page 130

# T-Bone
# Pickled in Red Wine

**STEFAN MARQUARD:**

*"This pickling is simply brilliant—and the T-bone comes out like butter."*

| | |
|---|---|
| 2 | **T-bone steaks, ca. 1 1/8" (3 cm) thick** |
| 2/3 cup (150 ml) | **Red wine** |
| 4 Tbsp | **Red wine vinegar** |
| 8 Tbsp | **Olive oil** |
| 2 | **Bay leaves** |
| 2 | **Tarragon sprigs** |
| 2 | **Thyme sprigs** |
| 4 | **Sage leaves** |
| 2 | **Onions** |
| 2 | **Garlic cloves** |
| | **Black pepper, ground** |
| | **Sea salt** |

Peel the onions and garlic and cut into small rings. Wash the herbs and pat dry. Stir in the wine, vinegar, and six tablespoons of olive oil. Put half the onions, garlic, and herbs in a bowl. Lay the steaks on them and cover with the other half.

Pour the marinade over them and marinate in the refrigerator for 12 hours. Take the steaks out, pat dry, and grill each side eight minutes over high heat. Season with black pepper and sea salt after grilling and let stand in foil for five minutes, then serve.

**Suggested sides:**
Grilled artichokes, see page 132

In a pan, add 1 min. per side to the grill time.

# T-Bone
# with a Breath of Mint

| | |
|---|---|
| 2 | **T-bone steaks, ca. 1 1/8" (3 cm) thick** |
| 3/8 cup (100 ml) | **Olive oil** |
| 2 | **Lemons, juice and zest** |
| 2 | **Garlic cloves** |
| 2 | **Rosemary sprigs** |
| 1 | **Thyme sprig** |
| 1 | **Bunch of fresh mint** |
| | **Salt** |
| | **Pepper** |
| | **Sugar** |

Put the olive oil, lemon juice, and zest in a mixer, add the garlic, rosemary, thyme, and the mint and mix it all. Put the T-bone steaks in a bowl, coat them all over with the marinade, and marinate in the refrigerator for two hours. Let the meat drip dry, season with salt, pepper, and some sugar, and grill each side seven to eight minutes over medium heat. During the grilling, brush repeatedly with the marinade. Let the steaks stand five minutes after grilling.

**Suggested sides:**

Grilled vegetables, see page 128

In a pan, add 1 min. per side to the grill time.

# Porterhouse Viva España

| | |
|---|---|
| 2 | **Porterhouse Steaks, ca. 1 3/4 lb (800 g) each** |
| 2 | **Garlic cloves** |
| 1 tsp | **Chili flakes, dried** |
| 2 Tbsp | **Sea salt** |
| 2 Tbsp | **Black pepper** |
| 3 | **Lemons** |
| 3 Tbsp | **Olive oil** |
| Some | **Dry sherry** |

Peel the garlic and dice, mix with lemon zest, chili, sea salt, pepper, and olive oil. Brush the steaks with this mixture and marinate in the refrigerator for three hours. Prepare the grill and grill the steaks six minutes on each side. Sprinkle more sea salt over them and let them stand briefly. Cut the steaks into slices about 3/8" (1 cm) thick and divide among the four plates. Finally, sprinkle a few more drops of dry sherry over them.

**Suggested sides:**

Devil's corn, see page 131

In a pan, add 1 min. per side to the grill time.

# Bistecca Fiorentina

| | |
|---|---|
| 2 | **Porterhouse steaks from a Chianina cow, ca. 2 1/4 lbs (1000 g)** |
| 6 Tbsp | **Olive oil** |
| 4 | **Rosemary sprigs** |
| 4 | **Garlic cloves** |
| 2 tsp | **Black pepper, ground** |
| 2 tsp | **Sea salt** |
| 1 tsp | **Fresh oregano** |

Chop the garlic and oregano small and brush the steaks with olive oil. Mix the garlic, oregano, salt, and pepper and rub it on both sides of the steaks. Lay the rosemary sprigs on them and marinate for 12 hours. Heat a grill pan very hot and fry the steaks in it for seven minutes on each side. Then let the steaks stand for 15 minutes in the oven at 175°F (80°C). Cut the steaks into strips about 3/4" (2 cm) wide at right angles to the bone for serving and divide among the plates.

**Suggested sides:**

Rosemary potatoes

# Porterhouse Toscana

| | |
|---|---|
| 2 | Porterhouse steaks at least 1 1/8" (3 cm) thick |
| | Olive oil |
| 2 | Garlic cloves, chopped fine |
| 2 | Rosemary sprigs |
| | Salt |
| | Pepper |
| | Sugar |
| | Sea salt |

Season the steaks with salt, pepper, and some sugar and grill at least seven to eight minutes on each side. After four minutes turn the steaks 90 degrees to form a nice grid pattern. Put the garlic and rosemary in a form that is big enough for both steaks. Take the steaks from the grill, put them on a dish, and pour olive oil over them liberally. Let the steaks stand for five minutes, turning them several times. Before serving, season again with coarse pepper and sea salt.

**Suggested sides:**

Scamorza potatoes, see page 126

In a pan, add 1 min. per side to the grill time.

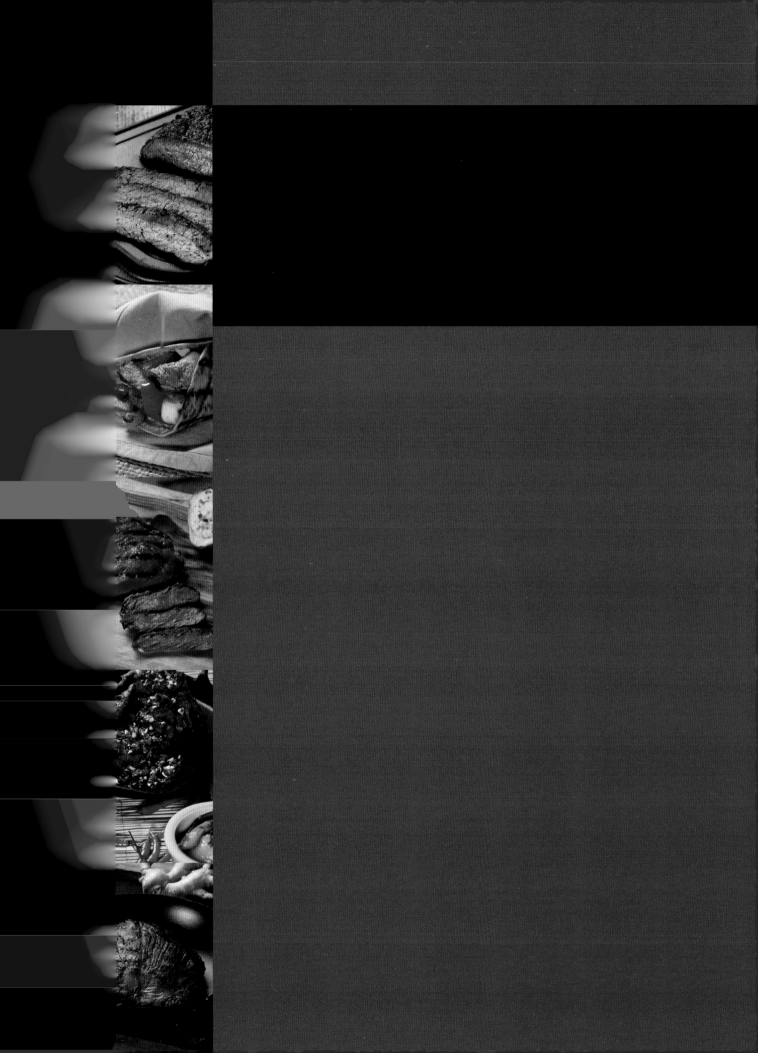

# EXOTICS

# BBQ Flank Steak

STEFAN MARQUARD:

"Be brave! With first-class meat, even something with coarse fibers works wonderfully as a steak."

| 1 | Large flank steak, ca. 2 1/4 lbs (1000 g) |
|---|---|
| 3 Tbsp | Brown sugar |
| 2 Tbsp | Paprika powder |
| 1 tsp | Cayenne pepper |
| 1 Tbsp | Mustard powder |
| 1 Tbsp | Garlic powder |
| 2 Tbsp | Dried basil |
| 1 tsp | Onion powder |
| 1 tsp | Ground black pepper |
| | Salt |

Mix the spices thoroughly and rub the steak evenly with them on both sides. Wrap the steak in plastic wrap and let it stand in the refrigerator for 12 hours. Prepare the grill for direct grilling at high heat. Grill the steak for eight to ten minutes on each side, let it stand five minutes in aluminum foil, and then cut it into thin strips for serving.

**Suggested sides:**

Devil's corn, see page 131

In a pan, add 1 min. per side to the grill time.

# Tri-Tip Steak

| | | | |
|---|---|---|---|
| 1 lb (400 g) | **Tri-Tip** | **For the Dip:** | |
| 1 | **Red pepper** | | |
| 1 | **Bunch pearl onions** | 3 Tbsp | **Tomato paste** |
| 2 | **Tomatoes** | 1 cup (100 g) | **Sour cream** |
| 1 | **Leek stem** | 2 Tbsp | **Sambal Oelek** |
| 2 | **Pepperoni, mild spice** | | **Sea salt** |
| 1 | **Red onion** | | |
| 4 | **Tortillas** | | |

Remove the seeds from the pepper and cut it in eighths, wash the leek and pearl onions, and cut the tomatoes into pieces. Grill the vegetables well and then cut into 3/4" pieces. Stir the sour cream, tomato paste, and Sambal Oelek to a smooth mixture in a bowl. Brown the tortillas briefly in a pan. Season the meat with pepper and grill three minutes on each side, then take from the grill, season with sea salt, and let stand in aluminum foil for five minutes.

Meanwhile, brush the tortillas with the dip and add the grilled vegetables. Cut the meat into thin slices and put on the tortilla, then roll them up, and serve.

 Brown the vegetables in a pan and add one minute per side to the grilling time of the meat if you fry it.

# Skirt Steak

| | |
|---|---|
| 2 1/4 lbs (1000 g) | **Skirt Steak** |
| 2 cups (500 ml) | **Orange juice** |
| 2 | **Onions** |
| 2 | **Garlic cloves** |
| 2 Tbsp | **Strong barbecue sauce** |
| 1 | **Piece ginger, ca. 3/4" (2 cm)** |
| | **Salt** |
| | **Pepper** |

Cut the onions, garlic, and ginger into thin strips. Season the steak with salt and pepper and put in a bowl, cover with the onions, garlic and ginger, and pour the orange juice over them. Marinate in the refrigerator for at least six hours. Take the steaks out, pat dry, and grill three minutes on each side over high heat. Then let the steak stand briefly and cut into thin slices.

**Suggested sides:**

Rosemary potatoes, or serve as sandwiches

In a pan, add 1 min. per side to the grill time.

# Chimichurri Skirt Steak

| | |
|---|---|
| 1 | **Skirt steak, ca. 2 2/3 lbs (1200 g)** |
| 2 cups (500 ml) | **Olive oil** |
| 6 Tbsp | **Red wine vinegar** |
| 2 | **Habanero chili peppers, without seeds, chopped small** |
| 6 | **Garlic cloves** |
| 4 Tbsp | **Fresh thyme, chopped** |
| 4 Tbsp | **Flat-leaf parsley, chopped** |
| 2 Tbsp | **Rosemary, chopped** |
| 3 Tbsp | **Fresh oregano, chopped** |
| 3 Tbsp | **Paprika** |
| 1 tsp | **Sea salt** |
| 1 tsp | **Black pepper** |

Warm the olive oil in a pot (don't let it get hot) and take off the stove. Add all ingredients except the steak and stir well. Let it stand an hour at room temperature.

Put the meat in a bowl, pour 1/4 of the chimichurri marinade over it, and let it stand at least two hours. Then fry in a hot pan ten to twelve minutes on each side. Let it stand for five minutes, then cut into thin strips against the grain. Serve the rest of the marinade with it.

**Suggested sides:**
Marinated pepper, see page 127

# Flank Steak London Style

| | |
|---|---|
| 1 | Flank steak, ca. 2 2/3 lbs (1200 g) |
| 2 | Red onions |
| 4 | Garlic cloves |
| 1 | Piece ginger, ca. 2" (5 cm) |
| 2 Tbsp | Coriander, chopped |
| 4 Tbsp | Teriyaki sauce |
| 3/8 cup (100 ml) | Red wine |
| 3/8 cup (100 ml) | Canola oil |
| | Salt |
| | Pepper |

Peel the onions, garlic, and ginger, cube, and put in a bowl with the coriander. Pour on the teriyaki sauce, red wine, and canola oil and let the steak marinate in it at least 12 hours.

Take the meat out of the marinade and pat dry. Prepare the grill and grill the steak 12 minutes on each side over high heat. Then let the steak stand in aluminum foil for five minutes. Cut into thin slices against the grain and serve.

**Suggested sides:**
Grilled artichokes, see page 132

In a pan, add 1 min. per side to the grill time.

# SIDE DISHES

# Scamorza Potatoes

| | |
|---|---|
| 4 | **Potatoes, firm baking variety** |
| 3 1/2 oz (100 g) | **Scamorza cheese** |
| 1 3/4 oz (50 g) | **Gruyère cheese** |
| 7/8 oz (25 g) | **Parmesan cheese** |
| 1/2 | **Bunch chives** |
| 3 Tbsp | **Whipped cream** |
| 1 1/3 Tbsp (20 g) | **Soft butter** |
| 1 Tbsp | **Coarse Dijon mustard** |
| | **Salt** |
| | **Pepper** |

Wash the potatoes, wrap in aluminum foil, and cook indirectly at 475°F (250°C) until they are soft (fork test). Remove foil, grill ten more minutes.

Meanwhile, cut the scamorza and Gruyère into fine cubes, grate the Parmesan fine, and cut the chives into tubes. Halve the potatoes and let cool. Carefully scoop out most of the potato flesh, leaving a 3/8" rim of flesh without harming the skin.

Mash the scooped out potato, stir in cream, butter, mustard, and Parmesan, making a smooth mixture. The hook on a hand mixer does this best. Stir in the scamorza cubes and chives. Season with salt and pepper.

Stuff the potato mix into the skins and grill until crispy on the rack for 10 to 15 minutes.

**Oven preparation:** Times are for cooking on the grill.

# Marinated Peppers

| | |
|---|---|
| 2 | Red peppers |
| 1 | Yellow pepper |
| 1 | Green pepper |
| 3 | Garlic cloves |
| | Olive oil |
| | Juice of one lemon |
| 7 Tbsp | Olive oil |
| | Sea salt |
| | Parsley, crudely chopped |
| 4 | Lemon slices |

Wash the peppers, halve, remove seeds, and brush with olive oil. Grill until the skin is black. Then put in a bowl and let stand covered for ten minutes. Peel off the black skin and cut the halves into even strips. Peel the garlic and slice thinly, mix with the lemon juice, some olive oil, and sea salt, and pour over the pepper strips. Garnish with the lemon slices and chopped parsley.

**Oven preparation:** Preheat the oven to 475°F (250 °C). Put the pepper halves on the rack or lay them on a sheet with the skin up, and leave in the oven until the skin turns black and makes bubbles.

# Grilled Vegetables

| | | | | |
|---|---|---|---|---|
| 4 | Eggplant | | Marinade: | |
| 4 | Potatoes | | | |
| 4 | Onions | 5 | Garlic cloves | |
| 4 | Zucchini | 1 cup (250 ml) | Olive oil | |
| 2 | Red peppers | 4 | Rosemary sprigs | |
| 2 | Yellow peppers | 3 | Thyme sprigs | |
| 1 | Garlic bulb | 1 tsp | Brown sugar | |
| | Coarse sea salt | | | |

Wash the zucchini and eggplant and cut lengthwise into slices 1/4" (5 mm) thick. Peel onions and potatoes and cut into slices 1/8" (3 mm) thick. Quarter peppers and remove seeds. Cut the top and bottom off the garlic bulb so it has two flat surfaces.

For the marinade, peel and press the garlic cloves. Mix the pressed garlic with the other ingredients. Put the cut vegetables in the marinade for two hours, turn several times. In aluminum foil, add the garlic bulb, pour on some olive oil, wrap it up, and grill 20 minutes over high heat. Then put the vegetables on the preheated grill and grill until a good grill pattern is formed. Arrange the grilled vegetables on a platter, press the garlic bulb and place cloves evenly over the vegetables. Drizzle the marinade over the veggies, add a sprig each of rosemary and thyme, and sprinkle some sea salt over them.

**Oven preparation:** Put the garlic bulb wrapped in foil in an oven preheated to 450°F (240°C) for 20 minutes. Fry the vegetables well in a pan.

# Tomato Grapefruit Mango Salsa

| | |
|---|---|
| 3 | Tomatoes |
| 1/2 | Grapefruit |
| 2 | Mangoes |
| 2 | Garlic cloves |
| 1/2 | Red onion |
| 3 Tbsp | Coriander leaves |
| 1 | Fresh chili pepper |
| 1 tsp | Rose paprika |
| 1/2 tsp | Cross cumin |
| 1/4 tsp | Cardamom |
| 2 Tbsp | Olive oil |
| | White balsamic vinegar |
| | Salt |
| | Pepper |

Peel the tomatoes, remove the seeds, and cut into small cubes. Fillet the grapefruit and cut small. Peel the mangoes and cut into small cubes. Peel the garlic cloves and onion, cube small, and chop the coriander small. Put all ingredients in a bowl, mix well with the spices, and flavor with balsamic vinegar, salt, and pepper.

Put the salsa in the refrigerator at least two hours to let it blend.

# Potatoes with Herb Sour Cream

| | |
|---|---|
| 4 | Medium potatoes |
| 4 Tbsp | Canola oil |
| 7/8 cup (100 g) | Sour Cream |
| 2 Tbsp | Crème fraîche |
| 1 | Small onion |
| 2 Tbsp | Chives, diced |
| | Salt |
| | Pepper |

Wash the potatoes well, halve lengthwise, and salt. Brush four strips of aluminum foil with canola oil and wrap the potatoes in them. Grill the potatoes indirectly at about 400°F (200°C) for about 40 minutes or put them in the oven. Peel the onion and cube small, mix them into the sour cream along with the chives. Add the crème fraîche, salt, and pepper and mix.

Open the wrapped potatoes, separate the potatoes somewhat with a fork, fill with the sour cream mixture and serve.

# Devil's Corn

| | |
|---|---|
| 4 | **Corn ears** |
| 1/2 cup (120 g) | **Butter at room temperature** |
| 1/4 tsp | **Cayenne pepper** |
| 1/4 tsp | **Chili powder** |
| 1 Tbsp | **Lime juice** |
| 1 Tbsp | **Parsley, chopped** |
| | **Salt** |

Mix the butter well with the spices and coat the corn with it. Add some butter.

Then wrap the corn in aluminum foil and grill indirectly or in a preheated oven for 20-25 minutes at 400°F (200°C), turning often. Unwrap the corn, coat with the remaining butter, and serve hot.

# Grilled Artichokes

| | |
|---|---|
| 4 | **Fresh artichokes** |
| 2 | **Garlic cloves** |
| 10 1/2 oz (300 g) | **Feta cheese** |
| | **Juice of two lemons** |
| 3 1/3 Tbsp (50 ml) | **White wine** |
| | **Ground black pepper** |
| | **Sea salt** |

Wash the artichokes, remove the stems, and cut off the top quarter. Crumble the feta and mix with the garlic. Put 1/4 of the feta mixture in each artichoke, drizzle with lemon juice, and white wine. Season strongly with salt and pepper and wrap firmly in aluminum foil. Grill the packets indirectly for 25 minutes at ca. 400°F (200°C), or put in the oven.

Unwrap and serve. **Caution: Hot!**

# Index

# Recipe Index

**Stephan Otto,** born 1966, made his passion his profession at the end of 2004, founding the OTTO GOURMET firm with his brothers Wolfgang and Michael. Trained as a banker and businessman, after long years as a business advisor, he went to the United States in 2001 and worked as a management advisor. At that time he became acquainted with American beef—especially the Wagyu-Kobe style sold by mail order—which moved him to give up his profession and enter the food business, exporting this fine beef to Germany.

OTTO GOURMET is very successful in finding and marketing exclusive, high-quality meat. Stephan Otto is dedicated to the strategy and commercial development of OTTO GOURMET, and thus has an important influence on the firm's products and customer service. It is his passion and inspiration to attract lovers of good meat. The durability of production, devoted breeders, proper animal treatment, and knowing the value of top-class gastronomy—those are the important criteria by which he chooses his products.

Stephan Otto is privately a griller.
"Roasting aromas from the grill, along with juicy, tasty meat, makes life worth living."

**Stefan Marquard,** star cook, is known for his creative, somewhat different cooking style. In the kitchen he likes to listen to punk rock music and sets the standard: "What tastes good is allowed—even if it sounds laughable at first."

Born in Franconia in 1964, he was trained as a butcher and then as a cook at the Hotel Rebstock in Wuerzburg. Jobs in renowned hotels followed as he spent a year on a culinary trip through Italy. Along with Adalbert Schmid, he opened the Taverna la Vigna, which very quickly became the best Italian restaurant in the German-speaking area. In 1991 he opened his first solo restaurant, the Drei Stuben in Meersburg.

With his unconventional style, he earned, among others, a Michelin star and 18 points in the Gault Millau. From 2000 to 2003 Marquard was the chief cook in Germany's greatest restaurant, the Lenbach in Munich. Since 2003 he has run Stefan Marquard's Event Catering with Wolfgang Weigler. Along with his team, the Jolly Roger Cooking Gang, he has bewitched all of Europe with his cooking skill, always true to the motto "cooking is like punk rock!" In 2010 Stefan Marquard opened two new restaurants, the Dining Range in the Olching Golf Club near Munich and a restaurant in the Bavarian Yacht Club of Munich at Starnberg.

**Steffen Eichhorn.** Born in 1976 in Franconia, Steffen pursues his passion for cooking and first-class food. When, by chance, he became aware of the Grillsportverein website, he had found himself. His grilled dishes became increasingly more elaborate, and finally he joined the master grill team of the Grillsportverein, winning a master's title in 2009.

For some time Steffen Eichhorn has not only worked closely with the OTTO GOURMET firm but also made his mark in barbecuing with renowned top-rank chefs like Kolja Kleeberg, Stefan Marquard, Peter Scharff, and Ralf Jakumeit. In 2009 he founded the BBQ & More firm, which offers event catering, grilling seminars, and dealer training for well-known grill manufacturers.

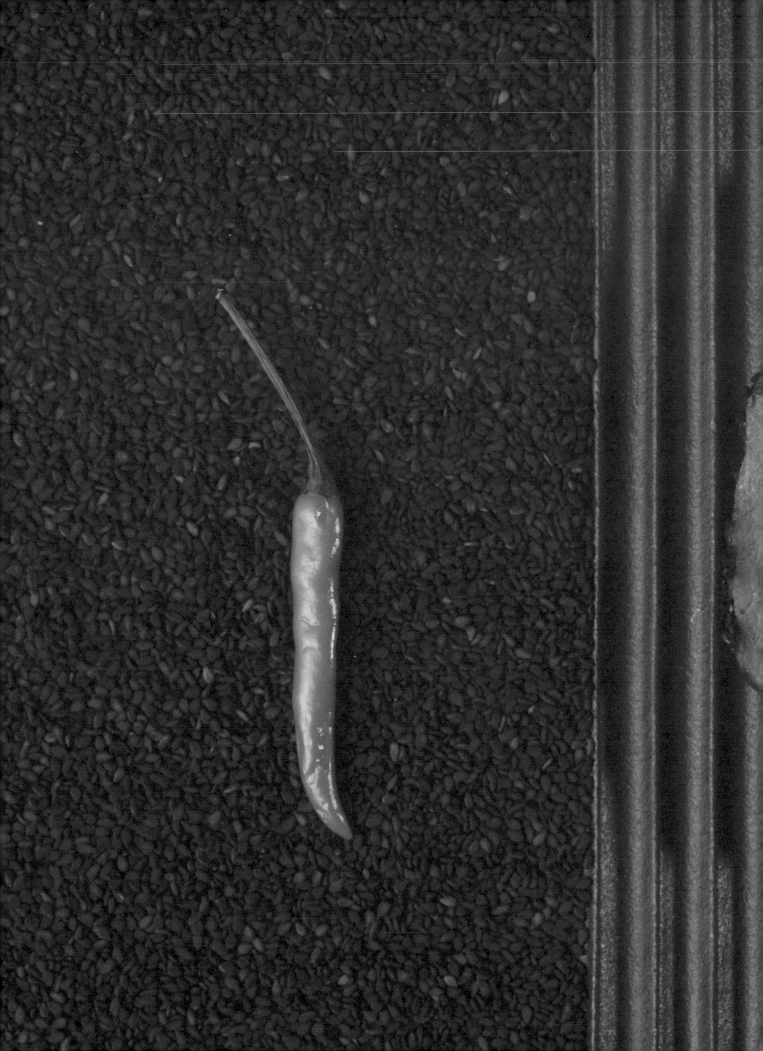